This book
belongs to

....

First Science Encyclopedia

Written by

Kate Scarborough and Philippa Moyle

Illustrated by

Teresa Foster

Contents

zigzag

What is science?

Look at the things around you. Do you know what they are made from and how they work? The people who try to answer these questions are called scientists. They study the world around them and try to understand it. This is science.

In this book, you will find eight different scientists who study their own science. They introduce themselves on this page.

There's so much to discover about the sea. In some places it is so deep that no submarine can reach the bottom.

Geologists study the rocks that make up the Earth. They also study volcanoes and earthquakes.

Chemists find out what things are made from by doing lots of experiments.

Scientists have made lots of discoveries and invented many things over the years. In 1879, Thomas Edison invented the first electric lamp.

Discovering something new can take many years of study.

Botanists study plants to find out how they live and grow.

Thomas Edison

Famous scientists

Aristotle was one of the earliest scientists. He lived in Greece around 2,500 years ago.

Galileo Galilei (1564–1642) was an Italian scientist. He is famous for saying that the Earth goes around the Sun instead of the Sun goes around the Earth.

How do scientists work?

Scientists do tests, called experiments, to find out what things are made from and how they work. Many scientists do their experiments inside laboratories, using expensive equipment. However, you can be a scientist and do lots of experiments at home!

There are many fun experiments in this book for you to try. Look out for the words **Try it yourself!**

Botanists use a microscope to study the structure of plants.

Microscopes

Many scientists use microscopes to help them with their work. Microscopes make tiny objects look much bigger, so that you can see them more clearly.

Bowl

Spoons

Glass

Plant

Mug

Tape measure

Paper

Magnet

Satellites

Satellites are spacecraft that circle around a planet in space. Satellites have many different uses. Astronomers and meteorologists use them for their scientific work.

Astronomers study the photographs of planets taken by space satellites.

These are some of the everyday objects you will need for your experiments.

Computers can be programmed to work things out for you.

Blindfold

String

Yogurt containers

Jar

Bean seeds

Computers

Computers are very useful to scientists. They can store lots of information that can be called up on to the screen at any time. Computers can be programmed to do many things.

Meteorologists use photographs taken by weather satellites to figure out what the weather will be like.

How your body works

Your body can do hundreds of things at the same time. You breathe and grow without thinking about it. How does this happen? The answers lie underneath your skin!

There are 220 bones in an adult's body.

Bones in the skeleton

Skull

Rib cage

Body records

The tallest person ever was Robert Pershing Wadlow who was 8 feet 11.1 inches tall.

The shortest person ever was Pauline Musters who was 24 inches tall.

The heaviest person ever was Jon Brower Minnoch who weighed more than 798 pounds when he died.

The oldest person ever was Shigechiyo Izumi from Japan who lived to 120.

As you get older you grow taller. You stop growing when you reach your full height.

Measure one of your parents, too. Are they still growing?

Measure yourself once a month to see if you have grown.

The skeleton

The skeleton gives your body its shape. It is made up of different bones. Bones are made of a strong, hard substance.

Muscles

Muscles hold your bones in the right position. They also pull on the bones to make your body move.

Your muscles get bigger as you exercise.

Your brain controls your breathing and sleeping.

Brain

Muscles in the body

Lungs

Heart

Digestive system

The brain

You use your brain to think. Your brain also controls everything that your body does.

Red blood cells

The heart

Your heart pumps blood around the body. Blood carries food to every part of your body. If your heart stops, you could die.

Heart

The lungs

Your body needs a gas called oxygen to live. When you breathe, your lungs take in oxygen from the air. The blood then carries it around your body.

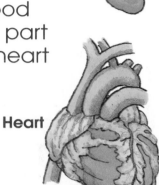

Stomach

The digestive system

You eat food to give your body energy. Food is broken down in your stomach and digestive system. It is changed to energy by cells in your body. Whatever is not useful is gotten rid of as waste.

Skin

Skin is a waterproof layer that covers the whole of your body. It keeps out dirt and germs. It also feels things that you touch.

Hippocrates

Hippocrates is known as the "Father of Medicine." He was born on Kos, a Greek island, between about 500–400 B.C. He traveled around Greece and the Middle East, teaching the people he met to look at the human body from a scientific point of view.

The body's senses

You use your skin to touch, your eyes to see, your ears to hear, your nose to smell, and your tongue to taste. These are the five senses. Your senses send messages to your brain, telling it what is going on around you.

Your skin feels things so that you do not hurt yourself.

Seeing

To see an object clearly, you have to focus your eyes on it by looking directly at it.

People who cannot see close objects clearly are called farsighted.

People who cannot see far away objects clearly are called shortsighted.

Touching

You touch things with your skin, which is very sensitive.

The pupil of an eye can grow as wide as 0.3 inch, or shrink as small as 0.05 inch.

Hearing

Your ears can hear many different sounds. Apart from your outer ear, the rest of your ear is inside your head (see page 26 for a diagram of the ear).

Your ears tell your brain where sounds are coming from.

Baa!

Moo!

The skin is one of the largest organs of the body.

Smelling

You smell things with your nose. Some smells are pleasant, but others are not.

Mmm...

Ugh!

Children have more taste buds than adults. Adults have about 9,000 taste buds.

Human senses are not as good as the senses of other animals.

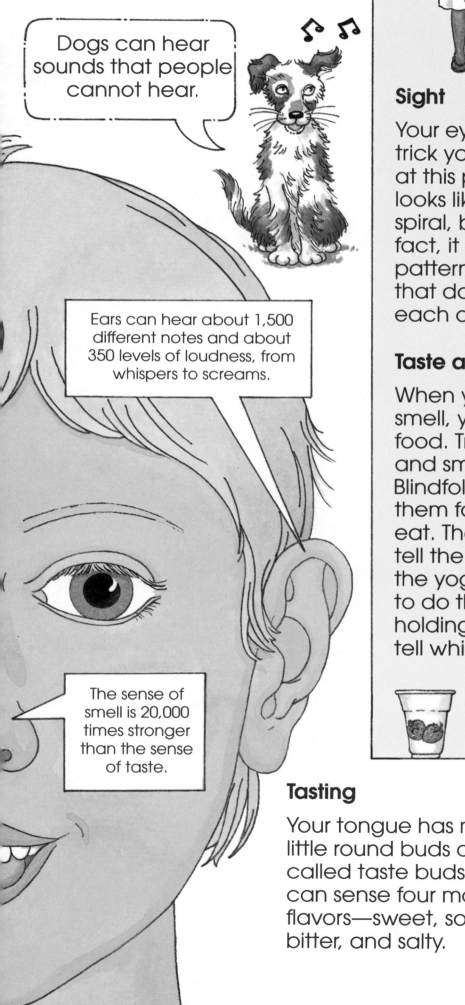

Dogs can hear sounds that people cannot hear.

Ears can hear about 1,500 different notes and about 350 levels of loudness, from whispers to screams.

The sense of smell is 20,000 times stronger than the sense of taste.

You can experiment on yourself to find out more about your senses.

Sight

Your eyes can trick you. Look at this pattern. It looks like a spiral, but in fact, it is a pattern of circles that don't touch each other.

Taste and smell

When you have a blocked nose and can't smell, you often find that you can't taste food. Try this experiment to see how taste and smell are linked.
Blindfold a friend and give them four fruit yogurts to eat. They should be able to tell the difference between the yogurts. Then ask them to do the same thing while holding their nose. Can they tell which yogurt is which?

Tasting

Your tongue has many little round buds on it, called taste buds. They can sense four main flavors—sweet, sour, bitter, and salty.

Potato chips taste salty.

This honey tastes sweet.

9

The world of animals

Scientists who study animals are called zoologists. There are about a million known types of animal in the world. There may be more that have not yet been discovered.

There are two large groups of animals. Animals that have a backbone are called vertebrates. They include mammals, birds, reptiles, fish, and amphibians. Animals that do not have a backbone are called invertebrates. They include arthropods, mollusks, annelids, and other animals, such as jellyfish and starfish.

Zoologists group together animals that share certain features.

Bat

Mammals

The bodies of mammals are covered in hair. Female mammals feed their babies on their own milk. Human beings, dogs, tigers, whales, and bats are all mammals.

Many large animals are mammals.

Elephant

Tiger

Dog

Frog

Frogs begin their lives as tadpoles. They gradually change into frogs.

Newt

Amphibians

Tadpole

Amphibians live half in water and half on the land. They usually lay their eggs in the water. Frogs and newts are amphibians.

Fish

Fish live in water. They are covered in scales, have fins, and lay eggs. Sharks and salmon are fish.

Shark

You can see if there are sharks in the water by their fins!

Salmon

Blue whale

Animal sizes

The **largest animal** is the blue whale. It can measure over 90 feet long and weigh over 100 tons.

The **largest land animal** is the African elephant. It can grow to over 9 feet tall and weigh over 5 tons.

Eagles can fly very high in the sky.

Birds

All birds have wings and are covered with feathers. Their young hatch from eggs. Eagles and penguins are birds.

Eagle

Penguins cannot fly at all.

Penguin

Earthworms make homes in the ground that are called burrows.

Reptiles have waterproof skin.

Earthworm

Snake

Lizard

Insects are the largest group of animals. They include flies, bees, ants, beetles, and butterflies.

Beetle

Spider

Arthropods

Arthropods have a skeleton on the outside of their bodies instead of inside! It acts like armor. Crabs, insects, and spiders are arthropods.

Mollusks

Mollusks have soft bodies. Most of them also have a shell. Snails, slugs, and octopuses are mollusks.

Snails have one large foot that they use to slide along.

Snail

Annelids

Annelids have soft bodies that are divided into many segments. Earthworms are annelids.

Crocodile

Reptiles

Reptiles are scaly animals that lay eggs. Crocodiles, snakes, lizards, and turtles are reptiles.

Turtle

Starfish

Jellyfish

Other animals

There are a few other small groups of animals that include jellyfish, starfish, sponges, and microscopic animals that you cannot see.

Sponge

One of the **smallest animals** is the dust mite, which is so small that you cannot see it. Dust mites eat dead skin cells that flake off your body!

The **fastest animal** on land is the cheetah. It can run up to 60 MPH over a short distance.

11

How animals live

Around the world there are hot, dry deserts, freezing cold regions, forests, oceans, lakes, rivers, mountains, and cities. Animals live in all of these different places.

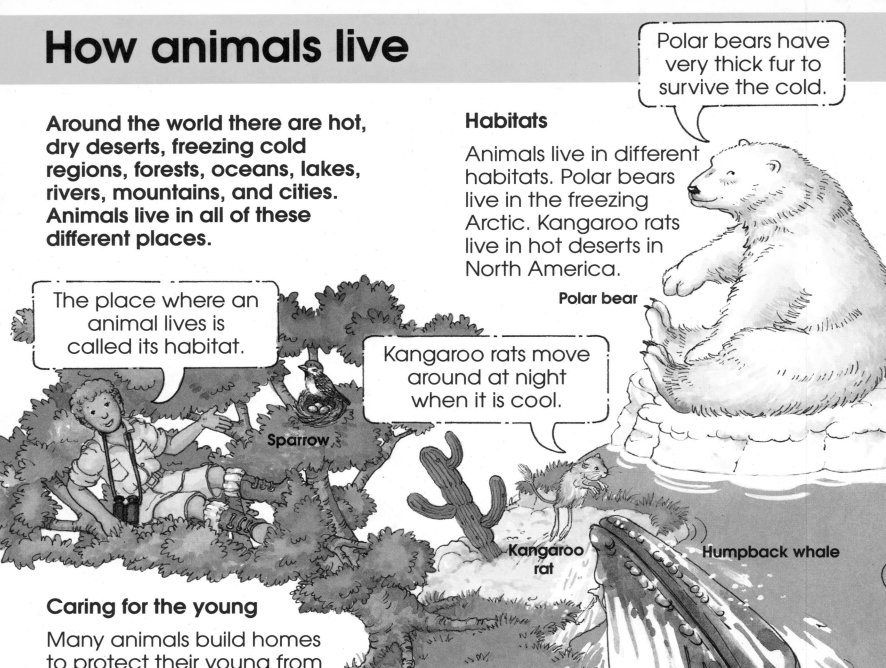

Habitats

Animals live in different habitats. Polar bears live in the freezing Arctic. Kangaroo rats live in hot deserts in North America.

> Polar bears have very thick fur to survive the cold.

Polar bear

> The place where an animal lives is called its habitat.

Sparrow

> Kangaroo rats move around at night when it is cool.

Kangaroo rat

Humpback whale

Caring for the young

Many animals build homes to protect their young from danger. Rabbits make burrows in the ground, while birds make nests in trees. Ants build mounds called anthills.

> Ants live together like a large family.

Ant

Rabbit

Animals in danger

Over the millions of years that animals have existed, many kinds have disappeared completely. They have become extinct. Dinosaurs became extinct over 75 million years ago. We know they existed because we have found their bones deep in the ground. Today, there are many kinds of animals that could soon become extinct. There are only about 200 giant pandas and about 50 whooping cranes left in the world.

Dinosaurs

Finding food

A few animals have amazing senses that help them to find food. Vultures have excellent eyesight that allows them to see something to eat from a great height.

Some animals eat only meat. They are called carnivores.

Vulture

Charles Darwin

Charles Darwin (1809–1882) is one of the most famous people to study animals. He traveled all over the world studying animals in their natural habitats. He believed that all living things are constantly changing, or evolving, over long periods of time to fit better into their surroundings. This changing is called evolution.

Some animals eat only plants. They are called herbivores.

Deer

Hiding

Animals hide themselves by blending their bodies into the background. Leopards hide in tall grasses while they hunt for animals to eat. Gray tree frogs are covered in a pattern that looks like the bark of a tree, so that they will not be seen and eaten.

Animals that hunt other animals are called predators.

Cheetah

Showing off

Some animals like to show off to attract a mate. Male peacocks display their fabulous tails. Humpback whales sing songs that can be heard hundreds of miles away.

Animals that are hunted are called prey.

Peacock

Gray tree frog

The world of plants

There are about 450,000 kinds of plants in the world. Scientists that study plants are called botanists. Botanists divide plants into groups in the same way as zoologists divide animals into groups. Botanists have discovered that there are some plants that have flowers and other plants that don't have flowers.

This primrose shows the basic structure of a flowering plant.

The **flowers** are often very colorful to attract insects. They may also have a lovely smell. The flowers produce seeds that will grow into new plants.

Flowering plants

Over half of the 450,000 kinds of plants in the world produce flowers. Flowers are important to plants since they produce seeds that grow into other plants. Flowering plants can be very large, like a horse chestnut tree. This produces large, shiny, brown seeds.

If you plant a horse chestnut it will grow into a horse chestnut tree.

Carl Linnaeus

Carl Linnaeus (1707–1778) was a Swedish botanist who invented a way of dividing plants into groups. He named nearly 8,000 kinds of plants and over 4,000 kinds of animals as well. He gave each one two names, which were in Latin.

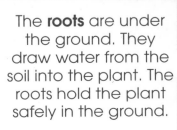

The **roots** are under the ground. They draw water from the soil into the plant. The roots hold the plant safely in the ground.

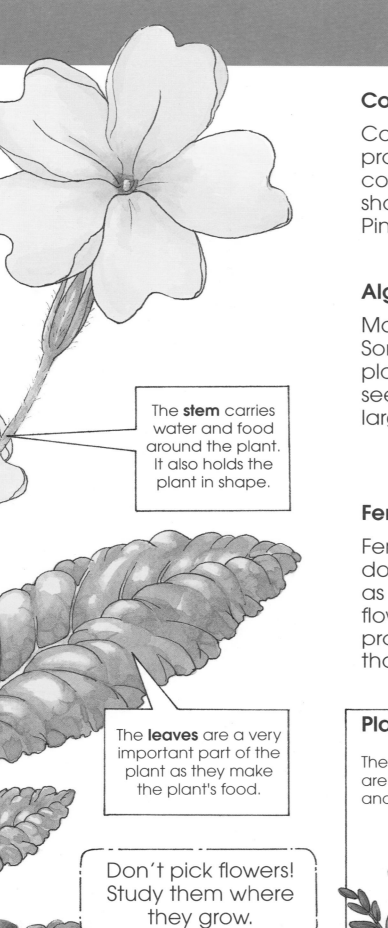

Conifers

Conifers are trees that produce their seeds in cones. Their leaves are shaped like needles. Pine trees are conifers.

Pine tree

Algae

Most algae live in water. Some of them are tiny plants that you can't see. Others are large seaweeds.

Seaweed

Ferns and mosses

Ferns and mosses don't produce seeds as they don't have flowers. Instead they produce tiny spores that grow into plants.

Fern

Moss

The **stem** carries water and food around the plant. It also holds the plant in shape.

The **leaves** are a very important part of the plant as they make the plant's food.

Don't pick flowers! Study them where they grow.

Plant facts

The leaves of a cactus are shaped like needles and are very sharp.

The flower of a bee orchid looks just like a female bee.

A clover has three rounded leaves. If you find one with four leaves, it is meant to be lucky.

Bluebells have flowers that look upside down, and the petals grow stuck together.

15

How plants live

As a year passes, you will **see changes** in the plants around you. **Plants grow quickly or slowly** depending on whether it is spring, summer, or fall. In winter, plants hardly grow at all.

In **spring**, leaves and apple blossoms appear on the branches.

Short-living plants

Some plants only live for one year. They are called annuals. Annuals grow from seeds in the spring. They flower in the summer, produce seeds, and then die.

Marigolds are annuals

Long-living plants

Some plants live for many years. Trees are a good example of this. Each year they grow bigger. After a tree has been cut down, you can tell how old it was by counting the rings in the trunk.

In **winter**, the leaves have gone and the branches are bare.

An apple tree during one year

Try these experiments to show that plants need light and water to grow.

Try it yourself!

To show that plants need water

Place a bean seed in a glass jar full of damp cotton balls. Put another bean seed in a jar full of dry cotton balls. Keep watering the jar with damp cotton balls inside but leave the other jar alone.

Bean seed with dry cotton balls

Bean seed with damp cotton balls

In **summer**, green leaves cover the branches.

Large flowers

The rafflesia plant in the Malaysian rain forest produces the largest and smelliest flowers in the world. They can measure up to 3 feet across and weigh up to 15 pounds.

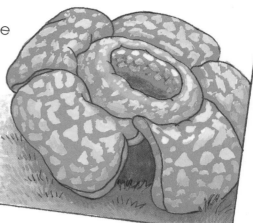

Plants are useful!

Plants make their food using sunlight, water, and a gas in air called carbon dioxide. This is useful because plants remove carbon dioxide, which is harmful to animals, from the air.

Food, medicines, and clothes

Plants are very useful to people. People eat plants, such as vegetables, and make medicines from herbs. They also use plants to make clothes. Many clothes are made from cotton that comes from the cotton plant.

Vegetables

Cotton

In **fall**, ripe apples hang from the branches and the leaves start to fall.

After four days, look at the seeds. The bean seed in the damp cotton balls should have grown a root. The one in the dry cotton balls should not have changed at all.

To show that plants need light

Cover both sides of a leaf on a green plant with dark paper. After a couple of days, take off the paper. You should find that the leaf has changed color from green to yellow.

What are things made of?

If you look around you, you can see objects everywhere. Outside, there are trees, cars, buildings, sky, and clouds. Inside, there are objects like chairs, carpets, and windows. What are they all made of? Scientists who study what things are made of are called chemists.

Solids, liquids, and gases are called the three states of matter.

Metal

Metal is a solid. When you touch metal it feels cold. You can polish it so that it becomes shiny. You can also paint it. Knives, forks, and saucepans can be made of metal.

Wood

Wood is a solid. When you touch wood it does not usually feel cold. Chairs, tables, doors, paper, and pencils can be made of wood.

Glass

Glass is a solid that can easily be broken. Windows, mirrors, and light bulbs can be made of glass.

Plastic

Plastic is a solid that is made by chemists. Some plastics are very hard and others are flexible. Bowls and bottles can be made of plastic.

Alchemists

Modern chemistry probably began in the 1600s. Before this time, the people who studied how things were made were called alchemists. During their experiments, they found that they could change things from one form to another. People believed that any metal could be turned into gold. A lot of people tried to do this, but no one managed it!

Solids

> Solids cannot change their shape.

You can move a television, but you can't change its shape. A television is a solid.

Liquids

> Liquids can easily change their shape.

You can pour water from a jug, which is one shape, into a glass, which is another shape. Water is a liquid.

Gases

> Gases do not have a definite shape.

The water vapor rising from boiling water is light and fills the room. It is a gas.

Water

Water is the most common liquid. Many other liquids, such as tea, orange juice, and milk, are mostly made of water.

Oil

Oil is a liquid that can be used for cooking. It is thicker than water. If you pour oil and water into a cup, they do not mix.

Air

You may think that the space around you is empty. In fact, it is filled with air. This is made from several different gases that you cannot see. One of these gases is carbon dioxide, which makes the bubbles in carbonated drinks.

Try it yourself!

Try this experiment to show that air is made of something.

Turn a glass upside down and push it down into a tub full of water. You will find that the glass doesn't fill up with water. Turn the glass to one side and bubbles will come out from it. These are bubbles of air.

Hot and cold

You know when the weather is hot because you can wear a T-shirt without feeling cold. You can find out how hot or cold it is by using a thermometer to measure the temperature of the air.

Temperature

Temperature is measured in degrees. You can measure it in degrees Fahrenheit (°F) or degrees Celsius (°C). A thermometer shows both the Fahrenheit scale and the Celsius scale.

The level of mercury in a thermometer shows what the temperature is.

Hot-air balloons

Air is made up of a mixture of gases. When gases are heated they take up more space and become lighter—less dense. This happens because the particles of gas move faster and spread out.

Try it yourself!

Some solids allow heat to pass along them to another object. If a solid warms up quickly it is a good carrier of heat. Try this experiment to see which solid is best at carrying heat.

1. Find three spoons —one metal, one wooden, and one plastic.

2. Put a tiny spot of butter on the end of each spoon and stick a frozen pea on to the butter.

Freezing water

When water freezes it turns into a solid called ice. Popsicles are made of ice.

> Water freezes at 32°F and 0°C.

Boiling water

When water boils it turns into a gas called water vapor.

> Water boils at 212°F and 100°C.

When the air in a large balloon is heated, the particles of gas spread out and fill the balloon. The air inside the balloon is now less dense than the air outside it, so the balloon rises into the sky.

Solids can melt!

Most solids will turn into liquids if they are heated to a high enough temperature. For example, a solid wax candle will melt into liquid wax when it is heated.

3. Put all the spoons into a mug of hot water.

Each pea will fall off when the spoon it is on becomes warm enough to melt the butter. Watch to see which pea falls off first. The first pea to fall will be the one that was on the spoon that was best at carrying heat.

Water

Plants and animals, including human beings, depend on water to keep them alive. Living creatures contain a lot of water. Nearly two-thirds of your body is made up of water.

Pure water has no color, taste, or smell.

How does a ship float?

Objects that are less dense, or lighter, than water can float. A heavy ship can float because its weight is less than the weight of water it pushes aside. You can see how this works below.

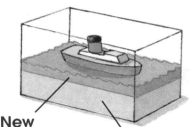

Water level

New water level   Old water level

The water that the ship pushes aside

Try it yourself!

Fill a bowl with water. Take two lumps of modeling clay. Leave one as a lump, and make the other into the shape of a boat. Drop both of them into the bowl and watch what happens.

Water turns into a gas

When you leave wet clothes on a clothesline, they slowly become dry. This is because the liquid water in the clothes becomes warm and turns into a gas, water vapor. This process is called evaporation—the liquid water evaporates into water vapor.

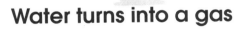

22

Exploring the sea

In 1690, Sir Edmund Halley invented a diving bell. This was a bell-shaped container that was used to explore underwater. Two people sat inside the bell. A third person swam outside collecting treasure from a sunken wreck.

Icebergs

When water freezes it turns into solid ice. Icebergs are huge pieces of ice that float in very cold water. Areas near the North and South poles have icebergs.

A gas turns into water

When you fill the bathtub with hot water the window mists up.

Some of the hot water evaporates into water vapor.

When the water vapor hits the cold window it cools down and turns back into liquid water.

This process is called condensation—the water vapor condenses into liquid water.

Try it yourself!

Make your own icebergs by putting some ice cubes from the freezer into a glass of water. Do they float or sink? They should float. This shows that ice is less dense than water.

Light

The Sun gives us light. If there was no light from the Sun, there would be no life on Earth, because plants and animals need light in order to live.

Day and night

We have day and night because the Earth spins around, making one whole spin in 24 hours. When the country you live in faces the Sun you have daylight, and when it faces away from the Sun you have darkness.

Light

Darkness

Shadows

If you are outside on a sunny day you will see your shadow on the ground. There is a shadow because light cannot travel through you. If you look around you will see that other objects have shadows, too. Light cannot travel through anything that isn't see-through.

Reflection

You can only see things when there is light. When you look at an object, such as a tree, what you really see is light from the Sun reflected off the tree.

> When it gets dark you use electric light to see things.

Colors

Light allows you to see the color of the things around you. When there isn't much light, they look gray.

Rainbows

Sunlight looks white, but a rainbow shows that sunlight is made of different colors. A rainbow forms when white sunlight shines through raindrops and is broken into different colors. Together, these colors are called the spectrum.

Try it yourself!

Hold a page of this book in front of a mirror. You are looking at a reflection of the page. What has happened to the writing and pictures? Everything is backward. When you look at your face in the mirror you see it backward, too. This is because the mirror reflects back exactly what it sees.

Sound

Sit still for a moment and listen. What can you hear? You may hear people talking, a car driving past, or an airplane flying overhead. These are all sounds.

Sound waves

If you drop a stone into still water, you will see waves travel out from it. Sound travels like this. When a sound is made, sound waves travel out from it. They are made by vibrating air particles. Vibrating means moving backward and forward very fast.

This diagram of the ear shows how you hear sound.

Sound waves hit the eardrum, making it vibrate. The eardrum is a piece of skin that stretches across the tube of the ear.

Nerve

Hammer

Anvil

Cochlea

Stirrup

Eardrum

Vibrations pass from the eardrum to three bones called the hammer, anvil, and stirrup.

Vibrations pass to the cochlea, which is full of liquid and has tiny hairs. The hairs send messages along a nerve to your brain, which understands the sound.

Try it yourself!

Stretch some plastic wrap over a round container and sprinkle sugar on top of it. Hold a metal baking tray above the container and bang the tray. You will see the sugar vibrate on top of the plastic wrap. Sound waves travel through the air, making the plastic wrap vibrate. This makes the sugar vibrate. The plastic wrap behaves like your eardrum.

The ear

Most of your ear is inside your head. The outer ear is the only part you can see.

Outer ear

The speed of sound

Native Americans used to put one ear to the ground to listen for the sound of galloping horses. They did this because sound travels faster through solids, such as the ground, than through gases that make up the air.

Echoes

If you shout in a cave, you may hear the sound more than once. This is an echo. Usually, sound waves travel out from a sound and don't return. In this case, the sound waves bounce off the wall of the cave and return to you.

Try it yourself!

You can make your own telephone and talk to a friend! Tie a plastic cup to each end of a long piece of string. If you talk into one cup and your friend holds the other cup to their ear in another room, your friend should be able to hear you.

Forces

When you try to move something you use a force. A force is a push, a pull, a lift, or a squash. A force can make something move or change its shape. You can see these forces in action, but there are invisible forces as well.

Pushing, pulling, lifting, and **squashing** are all forces.

Pushing someone can be quite tiring.

Squashing things changes their shape.

Magnets

Magnets have an invisible magnetic force called magnetism. Magnets pull some metals toward them. See which metals in your home react to a magnet. Don't try computers, video and audio tapes, or video recorders, since this will damage them.

The end of a magnet that faces south is called the south pole.

The end of a magnet that faces north is called the north pole.

Try it yourself!

Put a magnet under a piece of card and sprinkle iron filings on top. They will make a pattern as they follow the magnet's lines of magnetic force.

Lifting things can be hard work.

Pulling things along can be fun.

Backward and forward

Whenever there is a force in one direction there is another force in the opposite direction. For example, when you stop pushing something forward fast, you nearly fall over backward!

Gravity

If you jump off a park bench you won't fly up into the sky, you'll land on the ground. This is because the Earth has an invisible force that pulls you downward. It is called gravity.

A compass

A type of rock called lodestone contains iron that is naturally magnetic. About 2,000 years ago, lodestone was used to make the first compass. The needle of a compass always points toward the north. Explorers use a compass to find out which direction they should travel in.

Making things move

It can sometimes be hard work making things move. However, there are simple ways to make it easier for you. Here are some of them:

Levers

A lever is a simple machine that can make it easier to lift something. A seesaw is a type of lever. It is hard lifting a person heavier than yourself, but it may be possible to lift them into the air on a seesaw!
A seesaw balances on a pivot.

Try it yourself!

Ask someone who is heavier than you to sit at one end of a see-saw. You cannot lift them if they sit at the other end, but if you ask them to sit nearer the middle, the pivot, you may find you can.

Pivot

Gears

Gears are wheels with teeth. They can be used to make one wheel turn more slowly or more quickly than another, or turn in a different direction. On a bicycle they are used to make cycling easier and faster, so that your legs don't have to turn the pedals as quickly as the wheels turn.

Inclined planes

An inclined plane is a slope. Inclined planes make it easier to move things. It would be very difficult to lift a wheelbarrow full of earth, but it is easier to push it up a slope.

Gears make pedaling uphill a lot easier!

Gears are used in many other machines, as well as bicycles.

Moving in air

A bird makes flying through the air look so easy. But have you ever wondered how people and machines can move through the air? Studying shapes and air has made it possible for us to move in the air in all sorts of different ways.

> To understand how things fly, you must know that air pushes objects from all directions. Air is therefore pushing upward against anything that is falling. If a large, light object is falling, the air pushing against it can slow it down quite a lot.

Parachutes

A parachute has a large curved shape for the air to push against. That is why a parachute slows down as it falls. If you suddenly pull an umbrella down you can feel the air pushing up. But if you tried to use an umbrella as a parachute, you'd find that it would not work. This is because it is not big enough to support your weight.

Early flyers

The first successful human flights were made in hot-air balloons (see page 20). Two French brothers, the Montgolfiers, sent a hot-air balloon up into the sky in 1783. A hot-air balloon is known as a lighter-than-air craft. The first heavier-than-air craft to fly was an airplane designed and flown by Orville Wright in 1903.

Gliders

Warm, moving air rising upward can keep a glider in the air for a long time.

Kites

Kites are one of the earliest flying machines, dating back to 300 B.C. They only work on windy days, when the air pressure is high and can push more objects into the sky.

Try it yourself!

Air pushes against things. Hold a large piece of stiff card in front of you. Now try and run forward as fast as you can. It's quite difficult, isn't it? This is because the air is pushing against the card. If you hold the card the other way over your head and run, you will find it much easier.

The weather

What is the weather like at the moment? Is it sunny, cloudy, windy, raining, or snowing? The weather can be any of these things. People who study the weather are called meteorologists.

> When it is both sunny and raining, you might see a rainbow.

Sunshine

Sunshine heats the ground and the sea. Some seawater and water from lakes evaporates into the air—it becomes water vapor (see page 22).

Violent weather

A **storm** often has thunder and lightning, as well as heavy rain and strong winds.

A **hurricane** is a violent storm with winds reaching more than 75 miles per hour.

A **cyclone** is a hurricane where the wind blows ,round in a circle. The winds can reach 150 miles per hour.

A **tornado** is a violently spinning whirlwind that travels across the surface of the land or sea.

> If it is very windy, you may get blown off your feet!

Wind

Wind is moving air. The wind can blow gently as a light breeze, or it can blow strongly as a gale.

Clouds

Air containing water vapor rises high into the sky. The water vapor condenses into tiny droplets of water. Thousands of these droplets form a cloud.

Rain

The tiny water droplets in a cloud get bigger and bigger until they are so heavy that they fall to the ground as rain.

Climates

If you look at the pattern of weather in one place over a period of time you will find out the place's climate. There are several different climates around the world. The study of climates is called climatology.

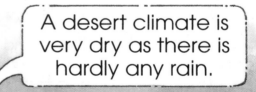

A desert climate is very dry as there is hardly any rain.

Snow

When it is very cold, the water droplets in the air freeze and fall to the ground as snow instead of rain.

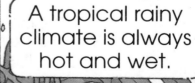

A tropical rainy climate is always hot and wet.

35

The Earth

The Earth is shaped like a round ball. It is a planet that circles around the Sun in space. Seventy percent of the surface of the Earth is water that is found in the seas and oceans. The people who study the Earth and how it is made are called geologists.

The Earth is made up of four layers—the crust, mantle, outer core, and inner core.

The **crust** is the outermost layer of the Earth. It is made of layers of rock. Its thickness varies from 4–5 miles under the oceans to 20–45 miles under the land.

The **mantle** lies underneath the crust. It is solid rock at the top, but deeper down the rocks have melted because of the heat. The mantle is about 1,800 miles thick.

The **outer core** lies underneath the mantle. It is made of hot, liquid metal and is about 1,400 miles thick.

The **inner core** lies at the center of the Earth. It is made of solid metal and is very hot—from 8,000–11,000°F.

Soil

The top layer of the ground is soil. Soil is made of tiny bits of rock, rotting plants, and animals. Plants and trees grow in the soil.

The longest river in the world is the Nile River in Africa. It is 4,100 miles long.

Facts about the Earth

The highest mountain in the world is Mount Everest. It is 29,028 feet high.

Rocks

Underneath the soil there are different types of rocks. Some are very hard, such as granite and marble, while others are crumbly such as shale and chalk.

This is a fossil of an ammonite.

Fossils

In some rocks you can find fossils of ancient plants and animals. Fossils show the shape of the hard parts of a creature that died thousands of years ago.

A changing landscape

The landscape of the Earth is always changing. For example, the waves of the sea wear away cliffs made of rock. This changes their shape so that the landscape looks different.

Volcanoes and earthquakes

Volcanoes and earthquakes change the landscape in a dramatic way. When a volcano erupts, molten rock called lava explodes into the air. As it cools, it forms a new landscape. Earthquakes make the ground shake, causing buildings to fall down. Whole towns can be destroyed by an earthquake.

The deepest part of an ocean is the Marianas Trench in the Pacific Ocean. It is 36,200 feet deep.

The biggest volcanic eruption took place at Tambora in Indonesia in 1815.

Space

If you look up into the sky on a clear night you will see the Moon and hundreds of twinkling stars. There are thousands of other stars and planets in space that are too far away for you to see. Scientists who study the night sky are called astronomers.

The Sun and its nine planets are shown below. Together, they are known as the solar system.

The universe

The whole of space is called the universe. It contains billions of galaxies, which are huge groups of stars, planets, and other space bodies. Our galaxy is called the Milky Way. It contains 100 billion stars!

The Sun

The Sun is a star. It is the nearest star to the Earth. The Sun gives the Earth its heat and light.

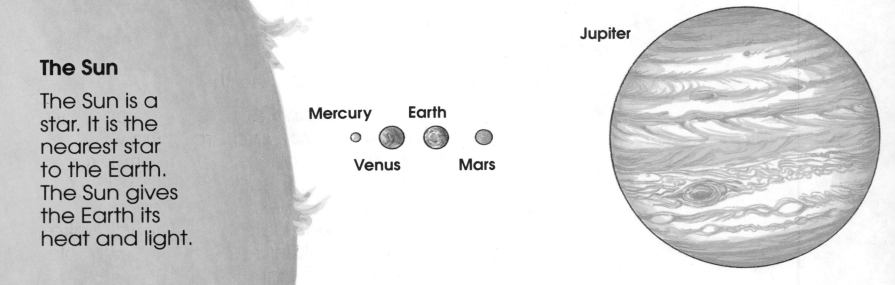

Mercury

Earth

Venus

Mars

Jupiter

Exploring space

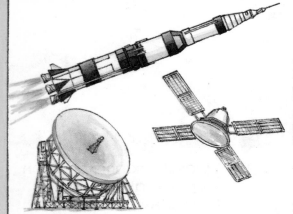

Astronomers use telescopes to look at the stars. They also send rockets, satellites, and probes into space to take photographs of planets. Although we know a lot about the universe, there is still much more to discover.

If you imagine the Sun about the size of a beach ball, the Earth would be about the size of a pea!

Stars

When you look at the stars twinkling in the night sky, they seem tiny because they are so far away in space. In fact, each star is a huge ball of gases that burns very brightly.

The distances between the planets shown below are not exact.

The Moon

Neil Armstrong

The Moon circles around the Earth. Neil Armstrong was the first person to step onto the Moon in 1969.

The planets

The Earth is a planet that circles around the Sun. There are eight other main planets in the solar system called Mercury, Venus, Mars, Jupiter, Saturn, Uranus, Neptune, and Pluto. In addition to these main planets, there are other lumps of rock in space called minor planets.

Saturn

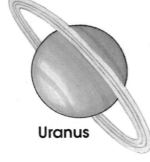

Uranus

Neptune

Pluto

Patterns of stars

Groups of stars make patterns in the night sky. These are called constellations. Ancient Greek astronomers gave these constellations names after their gods and myths. The constellation shown on the right is called Orion the hunter.

Index

Published by Zigzag Publishing,
a division of Quadrillion Publishing Ltd.,Godalming
Business Centre, Woolsack Way, Godalming,
Surrey GU7 1XW, England.

Consultant: Lillian Wright is a freelance Primary Science
Consultant and Curriculum Adviser for Science for the
London Borough of Hillingdon, England.

Editor: Philippa Moyle
Designer: David Anstey
Design Manager: Kate Buxton
Production: Zoë Fawcett
Series Concept: Tony Potter

Distributed in the U.S. by SMITHMARK PUBLISHERS
a division of U.S. Media Holdings, Inc.,
16 East 32nd Street, New York, NY 10016

Copyright © 1997 Zigzag Publishing.

Color separations by ScanTrans, Singapore
Printed by New Interlitho, Italy

ISBN 0-7651-9264-0